A Panda is Not a Bear

H.J. Bell

Presentation by *BookLeaf Publishing*

Web: www.bookleafpub.com

E-mail: info@bookleafpub.com

ISBN: 9789360942229

First edition 2024

*To Alyassa, my bestie and sister: no matter
what, no matter where*

*To Mathea, my lovely cousin whose support
and love is everything*

We Check Boxes

We check boxes before we even know what they mean. It becomes so ingrained in us that we don't even think twice about it.

We check boxes before we even know what they mean. My brother and I are 7 months apart. And for 5 months of the year we are the same age. In those 5 months we are the same, until it comes to boxes.
The first time I checked those boxes was at 7 in the doctor's office, seated next to my brother and mother as we registered for school. We were the same age, we shared the same home and name, but when it comes to those boxes, we were not the same. I remember my mother's sigh of shame as I checked the same boxes as him. How was I to know that the box "caucasian" wasn't meant for me? I silently cried myself to sleep that night as I learned that different was who you are and not what you want to be.

We check boxes before we even know what they mean. I remember the day I stopped checking the box "Chinese" for a language I spoke fluently. When had the words of my ancestors become forgotten and foreign to me? When had "ni hao" become the name of a kids' show and not a normal greeting? I remember going to sleep and no longer understanding what the woman in my dreams was saying to me.

We check boxes before we even know what they mean. I remember standardized testing when we had to declare where we were born. While my friends could check every box down to the minute of birth, I had but one. Every empty box left more questions with no answers. I remember hiding out at a friend's house because their mother had never seen the boxes I could never fill.

We check boxes before we even know what they mean. I remember getting my first passport. I remember every box that I checked led to more questions from the lady at the counter. "What is your ethnicity?" "Asian"…check. "Choose one" followed by a list of Asian countries, "China" check. Where were you born? China check. Where in China. Unknown check… I checked more boxes than my siblings and was reminded that different became a synonym for difficult.

We check boxes before we even know what they mean. College taught me many things. I remember applying for student loans and questioning if I met the requirements for the diversity scholarship…as an Asian adoptee in a German/Scottish/European midwestern family, living in a Norwegian/Scandinavian farming community, surely I did? I learned that I didn't check enough boxes. I would always be in the wrong box. To white for the Asians and to Asian for the whites. Which box do I check next?

We check boxes before we even know what they mean. Everything and everyone in a box. So we can see where everything belongs. But what happens when the box becomes a Russian nesting doll with you trapped in the very center. In the end we are all that last doll, squeezed into as many boxes as we can check. I don't want to check anymore boxes, be trapped in a definition that doesn't define me. Are we simply stuck in an endless cycle
of checking boxes before we even know what they mean?

Ghost

I want to hate you
But I don't know how
How do you hate a ghost
Is that even what you are
I used to wonder what I got from you
But now I think I know

The word abandoned holds no meaning
Or maybe it holds too much
Because every goodbye
Feels like a shot to the heart
The passing of time
Like the slow trickle of blood
Leaving my body through the wounds
You've left behind
And every hello
Like a breath of fresh air
Coming up from the water
After hours trapped under the surface

See I want to hate you
But I don't know how
Because of you I collect
Mental health disorders like Pokémon cards
You have Depression? I have it's evolution—
bipolar depression,

it comes with the power of suicidal thoughts
Dark moments I can't escape
Emotions? Don't even get me started
I'm as good at them as Ash Ketchum
Is at becoming the world's best trainer
Or maybe he's better
Cause 25 years later
I'm still broken by emotions

I want to hate you
But I don't know how
How do you hate something
without a name
See as a child I gave you name after name
Abba, Baba, Father
I wondered what I would have called you
I don't even remember what you look like

They say the brain is designed to forget what it
deems unimportant
I guess that's what you became
Cause I can still picture her
Hear her voice in my darkest moments
The language of my ancestors is embedded in
my brain
My subconscious remembers the sounds
But you are the biggest unknown
Sometimes I wonder if you were ever real

I want to hate you
But I don't know how
How do you hate a ghost
Is it even fair to call you that
Cause a ghost at least sticks around
I don't know if you abandoned me
Or if you never actually existed
I want to hate you
I really do
But I don't know how
Or maybe
I have all along

Colors

Colors are strange things. Mankind has defined and named a natural phenomenon and then used them to describe every aspect of life.

I remember the first time I was asked what my favorite color was. At 6 years old I always answered "orange." And while the other kids were asked why it seemed everyone was shocked that my little yellow tongue could wrap itself around such a word. As if the color orange belonged solely to those of white background.

Colors are strange. I've heard that if you repeat something enough it either loses its meaning or you start to believe it. I had said "orange is my favorite color" so many times that by the time I was 8 I believed it. When a teacher finally asked me why, the answer shocked them more than my ability to speak their language "because it was the only one left." In my large family everyone had a color, by the time I was brought into the family, orange was the only one that remained.

Colors are strange. We give things a color so that we can understand it better. They say that red is the color of love. The heart is red, blood and this life is red. That was what I repeated until it no longer meant that. To me love is yellow. Love, honestly love is life; what gives more life than the sun. That burning yellow ball of fire in the sky. The Russians use the sunflower as a symbol of love, it translates to "love from the bottom of my heart." That is the kind of love I want. I want the love of the color yellow.

I'm jealous of Edward Cullen

I'm jealous of Edward Cullen
The fact that he knows what others are thinking
Sometimes I wonder if that's a curse or a
blessing
Which is worse,
To never escape from others' opinions or
To never escape your own
To be slave to the madness that seeps into the
deepest parts of my mind
Leaving my brain darker than a new moon
Unable to see past the earth
To feel the warmth of the sun

I'm jealous of Edward Cullen
To be able to look in a mirror and see nothing

Never worrying about what others see
Or rather what they don't see
The broken pieces of a shattered childhood
The feelings of abandonment that leave a scar
Even the thickest skin cannot stop
A single word etched on the soul
Orphan is a state of being, a title that can either
tear a person apart
Or make them stronger than diamonds

I'm jealous of Edward Cullen
Who no matter his age,
never has to worry about what he says
Whereas every syllable that leaves my lips
Is ironed out to perfect
Every word carefully planned, like my bowties
Matched to every occasion
I tuck my thoughts deep in the waistband of my
mind
Praying my ducktail doesn't come out
I button up every opinion I own
Making the outfit of my vernacular
Palatable for your ears

I'm jealous of Edward Cullen

Balance

They say life is like a roller coaster
A series of ups and downs
But we are not park goers
Seeking thrills and laughter
Rather we are gymnasts,
Acrobats trapped on a tightrope
A careful balance between dark and light
Between Hope and demons
We search for a path
A safe way through the minefield
That is our memories

Half of My Heart

Half of my heart wants to get you
And half of my heart says don't be a fool
I try to be so casual
But lord knows I ain't that cool
Half of my heart says don't blow it
And half of my heart says you'll never know it
everyday that I see you
I never know just what to do
I thought I was so confident
But you see through it all
Even though I'm no party
You make me feel so tall
And half of my heart says don't blow it
Half of my heart says you'll never know it
Every time you talk to me
The future is all I see

Half of my heart wants it all
And half of heart just falls apart
Cause
Half of my heart wants to get you
And half of my heart says don't be a fool
I try to be so casual
But lord knows I ain't that cool
Half of my heart says don't blow it
And half of my heart says you'll never know it

Smile More Talk Less

Smile more talk less
Be nice say yes
Don't let them in it's for the best
Don't let them win it's just a test
Every word you say is their weapon
Every story let's them in
So build a wall
And make it tall
Never let them make you small
Most important of all
Smile more talk less
Be nice say yes
Don't let them in it's for the best
Don't let them win it's just a test
You taught me to be strong
Always learn to move on
All my insecurities
You pushed around like the leaves

You taught me what to say
Reminded me everyday
Smile more talk less
Be nice say yes
Don't let them in it's for the best
Don't let them win it's just a test
You never could believe in me
I always wondered what you'd see
Wanted to be perfect
What did you expect
Now that I'm free
To be completely me
Never have to
Smile more talk less
Be nice say yes
Don't let them in it's for the best
Don't let them win it's just a test
Now I've learned this
Don't need to smile just express
Be nice isn't always yes
It's ok to let them in, it's for the best
It's ok to let them win it's not a test
No need to
Smile more talk less
Be nice say yes
Don't let them it's for the best
Don't t let them win it's just a test
Smile more talk less
Be nice say yes

You

You are like a tornado
I see the wall forming, the dark clouds that are a
clear warning
It says batten down the hatches, take shelter
As the clouds grow larger and blacker, my
thoughts of you do as well.
It starts the same, rain that washes over
everything.
It's the cold kind, that chills you to the bone.
The winds pick up, making it hard to breathe
when it hits your face.
And then, in an instant it's gone. The world is
still quiet, deadly so.
The only sign you exist is the yellowish green
sky.

In an instant that calm is gone. Winds speed up
as a funnel of cloud comes tearing down the
street.
When you leave there's a pile of destruction in
your wake.
You may be the ones that created me
But that's all you'll ever be.
You left me abandoned and broken, like a town
after a tornado
Every time those memories or you are
mentioned, I'm back in that storm.
Like Katrina, Andrew, Ike, Camille and Wilma,
you cause destruction every time
You come around
When I think I've gotten over you, you return,
maybe with a different name
Buts it's always the same
I'm left with so much pain
More confused and alone than before
Every time I try to open up to someone
Those wounds you left open again
I can put bandaids on the wounds, board up all
my windows
But that destruction can't be stopped
That tornado is coming
The wall, the warning, it's just the beginning

I love you

I won't tell you I love you
Cause those words are used too much.
Instead I'll call you my antique watch
Because you are beautiful and timeless
As long as I have you
I'll always find my way home
I won't tell you I love you
Cause what do those eight letters even mean?
Instead I'll call you the moon to my ocean
The ebb and flow, yin and yang
Without one the other has no purpose.
I won't give you roses
Cause who wants love that has pain?

Instead I'll give you sunflowers
So you'll know I cherish you with every fiber of
my being
Don't tell me that you love me
Cause those words have been used as a weapon
Instead tell me your favorite superhero
So that I may know your soul
Don't tell me you love me
Cause those are empty words
Instead give me a hammer
So that I'll know you want to build this life
together
I won't tell you that I love you
But you'll always know it's true

A Name

Culture is a strange word in Webster, defines it as the customers, belief, social norms and material traits of a racial, religious or social group, but culture is so much more than that; it is an identity, a part of who you are, down to your very core
like a name it is both mundane and powerful the same time
but what happens when your name and culture are ripped from you and who you are is nothing more than a giant question mark
Shakespeare once wrote what's in a name that a rose by any other would smell just a sweet
but in many cultures the name is powerful and sacred. To know one's name is to control that person.

Rumplestiltskin hid his name, used it as a way
to gain favors.
My name carries more pain than power or so I
used to think
after all Dickinson once said Hope is a thing
with feathers that perches on the soul, but Hope
is a noun a feeling something will happen a
certain way
Hope: a noun to wish for something that could
come true, desire. Hope: a noun a thing or
person that will help one get what is wished or
desired

Hope: a noun to wish for something, believing
that it might be true or that it might happen.
Hope: a verb to want to turn out well.
Hope: a verb to dream, to aspire, to long for, but
Hope is more than that.
It's a feeling very deep within the soul longing
to be set free, but society is more powerful than
culture.
Society can strip one of their culture.
I remember being told that my culture wasn't my
own and yet years later, I was a target of anger
for not knowing my culture.
But to me Asian culture wasn't my culture, I was
raised on Disney and television. My first English
word was McDonald's, because what's more
American than that, my cousins, and I call

ourselves whitewashed because we have become
whiter than the rice our ancestors ate,
we would rather eat chipotle, than the food of
our birth nation
my little yellow tongue can no longer form the
words of the culture that was once mine. Instead
like a circus lion it has been whipped and trained
to speak the words of captivity.
The language of my culture is English, because
that is the culture of my social group. Asian
culture was no longer my culture. It was Asian
culture.
It was a China star on the street in my family. I
visited once a month. It was a failed attempt of
my friends and I had to copy the moves of kung
fu movies and the Power Rangers.
It was the ninja costumes my brother and I wore
on Halloween.
Asian culture is not my culture. It is Asian
culture.
My race and culture are no longer things to be
proud of,
they are the cage where my identity lies.
Race should be celebrated, not used as a
weapon. I don't want to be trapped in a race that
doesn't define me
a culture that I no longer understand.
The only race I want to be a part of is a race to
the finish line.

What if

I'm known for always talking, for having the
words to feel the empty silence but when it
comes to you I don't have a clue
See I know all the stories of a love that never
ends. I've seen the examples. I've read all the
books, but when it comes to you a single look
my way, gets me all confused
because I don't have the words to tell you how it
feels to get caught in the crosshairs. How do you
express a feeling that has always eluded you?
Some say it's simple, all the answers just seem
to line up but life is not like math. There is no
simple solution.
Confusion is a guarantee and no matter how
much I study I can't find the answers.
There's no such thing as wishing on a star and
fairy godmothers are few and far between.
Those childhood dreams, well, they don't get
you very far.
How do you express a feeling that has always
eluded you? How do you express love when it
never seems real cause I don't have the words to
fill that empty space and I've got awards for
speaking quickly, for knowing just what to say,
and how,

but when it comes to you the silence longer than
any road
from a distance, it seems easy, like blowing out
candles or catching snow
they say, it is as easy as 123 or even ABC and I
can start at the very beginning
it's the middle and ending that seem to cause all
the confusion
See I could sit and listen, listen to you all day
but to talk to you is a feat far more dangerous
than Frodo's trip to Mordor.
How do you express a feeling that has always
eluded you? How do you try something that's
never been a part of you?
How do you express love when it never seems
real when every time you think it's there it's a
ghost of your dreams.
I don't have the words to fill that empty space so
I play the 'what if' game.
What if I was brave like the superheroes in my
comics, facing aliens, with nothing, but their
pistol
What if I threw caution to the wind like Han
solo doing the kessel run or Luke facing Vader
with no training.
What if I was carefree like Winnie the Pooh
whose biggest worry in life was running out of
honey?
What if I told you how I was feeling,

what if you felt the same?
But what ifs are for children, for dreams and
stories that always have a happy ending they're
called fairy tales for a reason.
What if is a game that has no winners or losers
just a simple name.
What if is the biggest demon that lives inside of
my brain,
washing away all courage like sidewalk chalk in
the rain.
Because I don't have the words to tell you how it
feels to get caught in the crosshairs
To stare down Cupid's arrow to fall stupidly for
you, as if falling down the stairs.
For once in my life, I find myself at a loss for
words, unable to think of anything else when
you stare , and so I write,
because the act of putting pen to paper is easy,
those plain white pages; they lack the color of
your skin. Your bright eyes always full of
warmth, because as a story, the words come easy
like a knight slaying the dragon, I feel victorious
at least until the next time that I see you.

Fade to Black

I've always done what I should, been the good
girl, and held my tongue.
Knew when to speak, and when to run, play by
their rules.
I always try to keep my cool. So when is it my
turn?
Where's my happy ever after? That feeling,
we're all just searching for it.
That peace we all deserve. See, I've struggled,
and I thought, if I'm what they want, then what
do I do with every single little thought running
through my brain making me wish I was dead.
Human emotions don't make sense to me. I'm
like a vampire.
Lacking humanity pretending to be something
that I'm not. I've always been told what to do
and what to like.
Marry an Asian man. Have Asian babies like the
color orange because it's the only one left, be
grateful to be adopted.
This family is yours now.
But emotions cannot be dictated. So why do I
have to work hard every single day, just so that I
can say I'm doing okay when that's nothing but a
lie.
How can I be okay in a life that isn't mine?

I can find a thousand words to say, a song to describe my every emotion, but if you ask me what I'm feeling, I'll run faster than Usain Bolt being chased by a bear.

Emotions have never made sense to me. I use colors to show how I'm feeling, and yet no one seems to know what they mean.

The world says love is red like a rose, but what kind of love is the same color as power and destruction?

The Russians have it right. See, the Russians say, love, should be yellow like a sunflower. The Russian word for sunflower translates to love from the bottom of my soul.

That's the kind of love I want to feel, one that reaches every aspect of your being, stretching up to the sun, the very essence of life.

Instead, I'm left to wonder, do I even have a place here in this big world, or am I just some lost little girl with no home or family to call my own?

See, I've been told the color blue is the color of sadness and loneliness, but to me, it's always been orange.

The first time I said, I like the color orange, people were too shocked.

My little yellow tongue could wrap itself around the strange white word the first time someone asked me why?

The answer shocked them more because it's the only one left.

Orange has always been the color of loneliness for me, until you walked in the door in that burnt orange skirt.

See, I thought orange could start to mean something more. I let orange into my life.

It got closer to my heart than any other color before.

Forcing emotions to bubble to the surface like a boiling pot of water.

Only there was nothing to keep it from boiling over. Orange was far too close to red, burning everything that it touched.

Human emotions never made sense to me. Every time I experience them, the worse they hurt me. So when's it my turn, where's my happy ever after? That feeling, we're all just searching for that peace we all deserve.

Human emotions don't make sense to me. I'm like a vampire lacking humanity, pretending to be something that I'm not.

I've always been told what to do and what to like.

Marry an Asian man. Have cute Asian babies like the color orange, because it's the only one left, be grateful to be adopted. This family is yours now.

But emotions cannot be dictated, and eventually all colors fade to black.

A Panda is Not a Bear

A panda is not a Bear
No matter how hard one tries
They are separate creatures
You can change the panda's fur
Convince it looks like other bears
But it'll never be a bear

A panda is not a bear
You can teach it to speak
Sound like a bear
Lose its own voice
But it'll never be a bear
It'll still want to be with other pandas

A panda is not a bear
You can force it to act
Like all the other bears
Train it to perform
To blend in with the others
But pandas were meant to stand out
To wear their masks with pride

A panda is not a bear
You can force it to eat
The same foods as a bear
Convince it that it likes the taste of salmon

That it can survive on nuts and berries
But a panda will always crave
That crunchy bamboo
The food of its own kind

A panda is not a bear
Anymore than I can be
Something that you want

Chinese Barbie

You wanted the perfect doll
So you traveled halfway around the world
You chose the one you thought
Would be the best for you
Instead you got the broken one
You wanted the perfect doll
One that you could dress up
Coddle and mold the way you want
You wanted a Barbie
Instead you got Chinese Barbie

See Barbie is perfect
You can dress her anyway
Brush her hair, no scars anywhere
Chinese Barbie is different

You can't dress her the way you want
She prefers no hair, her scars are a tapestry
They tell the story she no longer
Has the words for

You wanted the perfect doll
Instead you got the broken and discarded one
The one that no one wanted
The one with secrets and fears
You wanted a doll that could be anything
But Chinese Barbie doesn't have that courage
Chinese Barbie lives in fear

You wanted a clean slate
A chance to mold a person into your ideal
Instead you got Chinese Barbie
Who already has dreams
Not of who she'll be
But of who she was

You wanted the perfect doll
So you traveled halfway around the world
You had dreams and desires
Hopes and wishes for the future
Instead you got Chinese Barbie
Who has more questions than answers
Whose hopes and wishes are in the past
You wanted the perfect doll
But what do you have now?

Abandoned

In the darkness of my deepest fears,
Lies a shadow that whispers, softly sears.
Fear of abandonment, a haunting cloak,
An ache that clings, a relentless yoke.

Within my heart, a fragile flame,
Yearns for love, fears its own name.
A dance of doubts, an anxious refrain,
Ebbing and flowing, a never-ending pain.

Oh, how it slithers, this fear so cold,
Its tendrils constrict, a story untold.
Whispering doubts, stitching seams of doubt,
Shaking the foundation that love brought about.

But amidst this tempest, a glimmer of might,
A flicker of hope, a celestial light.
For in vulnerability, strength is born,
A truth to be found, a rose with thorns.

I shall rise above this fear's cruel guise,
With open heart and searching eyes.
For true love conquers, it soothes the soul,
Breaks through the fear and makes us whole.

So, fear of abandonment, I shall not yield,

I'll embrace the unknown, let my heart be healed.
For in the face of this fear's vile shade,
I'll find the courage, the love, the grace in the brokenness

Childhood Crushes

In the realm of innocence and wonder,
Where hearts dance to the beat of thunder,
I shall unveil a tale of tender plight,
A symphony of emotions, pure and bright.

Oh, childhood crush, a bittersweet delight,
A flower blossoming, bathed in sunlight.
With flushed cheeks and timid smiles,
We set sail on innocent dreams' isles.

Like butterflies fluttering in the spring,
A newfound feeling begins to cling,
A gentle whisper in the depths of our being,
A secret adorned with grace, so freeing.

In playgrounds, we played our charade,
Chasing laughter like a hidden cascade.
In stolen glances, secrets we shared,
Fanning a flame that in our hearts flared.

Oh, the innocence of love's first bloom,
A kaleidoscope of colors in our little room.
With every passing day, our bond grew,
Like fragile petals kissed by morning dew.

Yet, as childhood winds began to fade,

Reality's curtain drew back, unswayed,
Our worlds, once entwined, began to part,
Like fragile fragments engraved in our heart.

But let us cherish those days of yore,
When our souls danced, forevermore,
For childhood crushes, forever they stay,
Memories etched in time, come what may.

So, let us reminisce, dear friend,
On childhood's crushes, that sweet trend,
For in those moments, pure and divine,
We learned how love's enchantment can shine.

Dreams

In the realm of golden hues, where innocence resides,
Where dreams take flight on fanciful rides,
There exists a place, in memories enshrined,
Where childhood dreams once intertwined.

In the meadows of imagination, as flowers bloom,
Where endless possibilities dispel all gloom,
Roaming barefoot, through enchanted woods I'd tread,
With dreams unfettered, a crown upon my head.

I'd drift through skies, on wings of paper and string,
Dancing with clouds, where imagination took wing,
A pirate, an astronaut, a wondrous explorer,
Every dream a gateway to worlds much grander.

In whispers of moonlit nights, secrets would unfurl,
As stars whispered tales, my heart would twirl,
Captivated by the wonders that lay beyond my sight,
I'd lose myself in dreams, embracing the night.

A castle of cardboard, a masterpiece unbound,
With crayons and brushes, my kingdom I'd
surround,
Creating magnum opus on walls made of
dreams,
Where colors exploded, and life burst at the
seams.

But times changed, as they always do,
And realities obscured the dreams I once knew,
Yet deep within still lingers the hopes and
desires,
The embers of childhood, fueled by eternal fires.

For within those dreams, still lies a key,
Unlocking the essence of who I'm meant to be,
They teach me to remember the power of the
mind,
To embrace the child within, and leave the world
behind.

So, let us cherish those childhood dreams,
For they illuminate life's dimly lit seams,
Let their magic guide us with each passing day,
And keep the spirit of wonder forever at play.

Escape in Comics

In vibrant panels, worlds take shape,
Where ink and brush bring heroscape.
Through vivid colors, tales are told,
Where hearts find solace, dreams unfold.

Escape we seek in comics' embrace,
To wander realms without a trace.
Beneath the mask, we find release,
In pages filled with endless peace.

Inked upon the canvas, heroes rise,
With powers bold and fearless eyes.
They leap through time, break cosmic chains,
Defying limits, shattering constraints.

From Gotham's streets to galaxies far,
We soar on wings and warp through stars.
With every turn, we leave behind,
The weight of burdens, tangled mind.

In tales of triumph, villains dance,
Their dark allure invites a chance,
To witness conflict, battles fought,
Where right meets wrong, lines are blurred.

But in the end, heroes arise,

With courage forged from the deepest skies.
Their strength, a beacon in the night,
Guiding lost souls toward the light.

Escape we find in these parallel plains,
Where journeys end and start again.
Through simple frames, enchantment flows,
Unveiling truths only the heart knows.

So let us wander, page by page,
Within this refuge, let us engage.
For in comics true, we find our kind,
A sanctuary for both heart and mind.

Ghosts and Demons

In the depths of my mind, a chilling sight
Ghosts and demons take flight
Their whispers echo through my brain
A haunting refrain

Their presence I can't ignore
A constant, gnawing score
Their whispers never cease
A maddening tease

They taunt and they play
In the shadows of my day
Their mischief never fades
A never-ending shade

But I know I must be strong
And push them back where they belong
For in the light of day
They lose their sway

So I'll face them head on
And chase them away
For in the light of love
They have no sway

Lost Dreams

In slumber's embrace, I find my heart's reprieve
Lost dreams, like shadows, dance within my
mind's eye
Their whispers echo loud, a haunting melody
A symphony of what could have been, left
behind

Their memories linger, a bittersweet refrain
A longing for a life that could have been gained
Their absence, a void that cannot be filled
A sorrow that my soul cannot be still

Their laughter and tears, a distant memory
A fleeting glimpse of what could have been, a
fantasy
Their dreams, like mine, were once so bright and
bold
Now lost, like shards of glass, forever cold

Their footsteps fade, like the setting sun
Leaving me with memories, now so dim and
done
Their dreams, like mine, were once so full of life
Now lost, like shadows, in the endless strife

A House not a Home

In a world of brick and timber,
Stands a house, once full of shimmer,
But its walls now echo silence,
A dwelling lost in bleak defiance.

Once a structure filled with laughter,
Now whispers graze deserted rafters,
Windows peer into barren rooms,
Where emptiness and sadness loom.

Within these walls, secrets reside,
Aching memories they try to hide,
The empty chairs, the vacant spaces,
Echoes of love that left no traces.

The hearth, once a source of warmth,
Now bears the burden of desertion's sword,
The fireplace, void of flickering glow,
No longer a beacon to guide souls.

The walls, adorned with framed snapshots,
Now relics of a love's aftermath,
Like distant echoes of once-tread floors,
Forgotten footprints at locked doors.

A house that shelters, yet fails to hold,

A home, it yearns to break the mold,
For bricks and mortar cannot make,
A sanctuary when hearts forsake.

Oh, house of walls, so tall and grand,
With empty rooms that cannot understand,
The nightfall steals away your dreams,
Leaving only echoes of faded seams.

But still, hope lingers in the air,
A whisper, a prayer for souls to repair,
May a lost house one day find its worth,
Transforming walls into a home's rebirth.

Family

I always wondered what family was,
cause where I was had more
questions than love.
I was told that family loved you
no matter what
and yet where I was
left me wondering
where was that love.
I'd been told who I was
that my name meant
girl waiting,
Is that all I'd ever be?
Just waiting in the wings
for acceptance
that'd never be.

But fate had other plans
It put me in your path
forced a connection
that wouldn't happen otherwise.
From simple conversations
to silly jokes
a friendship was formed
far greater than the bonds of blood.
You became more to me
than the love that'd never be

Family is more than blood,
More than love
With you I learned the real meaning
of who I am
See my name means
Precious memories
and each one made with you
reminds me that
chosen family
was always meant to be

From chance encounters
to international conversations
acceptance was found
in my cheetah sister.
I understand what family means now
because no matter what
no matter where
I thank fate
that you will be there

Sister

In this world, where bonds are rare,
A best friend like a sister, beyond compare,
Through laughter and tears, hand in hand,
A connection so strong, forever we stand.

Like a beacon, guiding through life's haze,
With understanding eyes, and comforting ways,
You know my secrets, my fears, my dreams,
A confidante, through every twist and theme.

We share the same heartbeat, intertwined,
Unbreakable, this friendship, eternally bind,
In each other's presence, we find solace and
peace,
A love that grows, never to cease.

Through the sunshine and storms, we weather so
strong,
A sisterly love, forever lifelong,
You lift me up when I'm feeling low,
With a simple touch, you let me know.

You're the one I turn to, in times of need,
A shoulder to lean on, with remarkable speed,
Our souls dance in harmony, forever entwined,
A friendship so precious, one of a kind.

So here's to you, my sister-like friend,
Through thick and thin, till the very end,
You are my rock, my guiding light,
A best friend, more like a sister, holding me tight.

Possibilities

In the realm of dreams, a thousand thrives,
Where endless paths, divergent lives,
A tapestry woven, bold and bright,
With myriad hues that dance in light.

A thousand stars in the midnight sky,
Each one a chance to spread wings and fly,
Possibilities, shining so vast,
A universe of futures, shadows cast.

In every whisper, a new desire,
A thousand paths, like sparks of fire,
From gentle whispers to thunderous roars,
A symphony of dreams, forevermore.

In the blink of an eye, a thousand doors,
Awaiting with secrets, treasures, and more,
A world of choices, awaiting embrace,
A thousand different destinies to chase.

Each step we take, a new direction,
A thousand ways to shape our reflection,
In the tapestry of life, we find,
A thousand possibilities, intertwined.

So embrace the unknown, with open heart,

For a thousand different possibilities, you are a part,
In every moment, a chance to explore,
A thousand paths, forevermore.

What is love?

Love is not to be taken lightly. Our parents are the ones that teach us how to love. My mother taught me that love is not free. My mother taught me to fear. That sometimes the people that are supposed to love us the most are the ones that cause the most pain. I've hidden the most important detail about me because of this life lesson. My father taught me that love is unconditional. He showed me that sometimes the one who never wanted you is the one that loves you the most. I've harbored feelings, authentic feelings for a woman for 7 years because of this lesson. My mother taught me that love comes with a price. Perfect was the only way to be seen, much less loved. I've been afraid to admit my feelings for years because that was not perfect. My father taught me that love has no strings. The only thing that has strings are toys and one does not play with love. I believe in commitment disputes never being in a serious relationship because of this. Our parents teach us the meaning of love, to me love might be bipolar. At the end of the day love is something that is unexplainable and necessary in order to survive. One day I'll be able to love everything, one day I'll be able to express love to the one I have loved for years.

Can We Go Back?

Can we go back
Back where it all began
Back before I was seven
Where we laughed and played
Where nothing was wrong
Where happiness was a song
I have so much to say
But everything gets lost
And every new day
Brings me more pain
I want to tell you
How you have hurt me
How you helped me to grow
And all the lessons I learned
Make me me even though
You'll never know the truth
Can we go back

back to a time

when nothing mattered

where trust was easy

and dreams had a chance

Who are you?

Where is the peace that passes understanding?
The love never failing
The joy unending
And the life everlasting?
I've heard the stories
I know all the words.
They say you wipe away the tears
Bring joy to those around.
Your grace moves mountains
And your spirit heals
But can it heal this broken one?
How can you be as great as they say
Yet remain the man they nailed to that cross.
Are you just a symbol
Meant to shine a light?
Are you even real
Or was it all a tale told in the night?
Where is the light in the darkness?
The calm in the storm?
They say you calmed the seas,
Can you calm the ones in me?
They say you move mountains
And bring the dead to life.
If you have this much power
Why is there still strife?
How can you be as great as they say
Yet remain the man they nailed to that cross.

Are you just a symbol
Meant to shine a light?
Are you even real
Or was it all a tale told in the night?

I Hear a Voice

In the darkness
In the ticking of the clock
In the silence
In the stillness of the night
I hear a voice
It's calling out to me
It says I'm loved
It says I'm free
I hear that voice
And I wonder if it's real
The things it says like
I am chosen
I am wanted
Not abandoned or alone
And I say
I wanna believe
In the things I hear
I wanna see
The truths of the words
I wanna know
The peace of your grace
In the chaos
Of the people all around
In the noise
Of the world I'm in
I hear a voice
It's calling out to me

It says I'm loved
It says I am free
I hear that voice
And I wonder if it's real
The things it says like
I am not broken
I have a purpose
There is more out there than this
And I say
I wanna believe
In the things I hear
I wanna see
The truths of the words
I wanna know
The peace of your grace
In the hurting
Surrounding my heart
In the fear
Taking over my brain
I hear a voice
Calling out to me
It says I'm loved
Says I am free
I hear that voice
And I wonder if it's real
The things it says like
I am important
I'm not forgotten
Not just a part of the crowd

And I say
I wanna believe
In the things I hear
I wanna see
The truths of the words
I wanna know
The peace of your grace
In the sorrow
Cutting through my soul
In the misery
In every face I see
I hear a voice
Calling out to me
It says I'm loved
It says I am free
In the despair
Living deep within me
In the confusion
Wreaking havoc on my brain
I hear a voice
It's getting louder everyday
I hear a voice
Trying to speak with me
I hear a voice
Desperate to connect
I hear a voice
I hear a voice
I hear your voice
You say that it's real

All the things I hear
You say it's true
All the words whispered in the night
You say it's real
The peace of your grace
And I say
I wanna believe
In the things I hear
I wanna see
The truths of the words
I wanna know
The peace of your grace
And I say
Teach me to believe
In the things I hear
Teach me to see
The truths of your words
Teach me to know
The peace of your grace
Cause I wanna hear that voice
Wanna hear your voice
In the darkness
In the ticking of the clock
In the silence
In the stillness of the night
I hear a voice
It's calling out to me
I hear a voice
You're calling out to me

Fly

Saying I believe
Is like saying I can fly
It's easy to do
But hard to prove
Like a baby bird
I flap my wings and hop around
Waiting for the wind
To lift me up